P9-DCQ-547

# DOGS ON THE JOB!

### True Stories
### of Phenomenal Dogs

**ALSO BY CHRISTOPHER FARRAN**

ANIMALS TO THE RESCUE!

# DOGS ON THE JOB!

## True Stories of Phenomenal Dogs

**CHRISTOPHER FARRAN**

**ILLUSTRATED BY PAT BAILEY**

AVON BOOKS

*An Imprint of HarperCollinsPublishers*

Dogs on the Job!
Copyright © 2003 by Christopher Farran
Illustrations copyright © 2003 by Pat Bailey
All rights reserved. No part of this book may be reproduced in any
manner whatsoever without written permission except in the case of
brief quotations embodied in critical articles or reviews.
Printed in the United States of America.
For information address HarperCollins Children's Books, a division of
HarperCollins Publishers, 1350 Avenue of the Americas, New York, NY 10019.

Library of Congress Cataloging-in-Publication Data
Farran, Christopher, 1942–
   Dogs on the job! : true stories of phenomenal dogs / Christopher Farran ; illustrated by
Pat Bailey. — 1st Avon ed.
      p.    cm.
   Summary: a collection of true stories of animals that work for a living, including Alaskan
sled dogs, bomb-sniffing dogs, and canine movie stars.
   ISBN 0-06-441102-8 (pbk.)
   1. Working dogs—United States—Anecdotes—Juvenile literature.  [1. Working dogs—
Anecdotes.  2. Dogs—Anecdotes.]  I. Bailey, Pat, 1948–  ill.  II. Title.
SF428.2.F27   2003                                                                   2002006514
636.73—dc21                                                                                 CIP
                                                                                             AC

First Avon edition, 2003

AVON TRADEMARK REG. U.S. PAT. OFF. AND IN OTHER COUNTRIES,
MARCA REGISTRADA, HECHO EN U.S.A.
❖
Visit us on the World Wide Web!
www.harperchildrens.com

**For Jack and Cathy Clark,
with love and admiration**

# Contents

# INTRODUCTION: WHAT'S WORK TO a DOG?

What do *you* consider work?

Homework? Yardwork?

Cleaning up that three-ring circus you call a bedroom?

Whatever it is, we're pretty sure that dogs don't have the concept—the idea—of work. If dogs don't have an idea of what work is, what do *we* consider work for a dog? Bringing the newspaper into the house in the morning? That's a useful activity, but it hardly qualifies as work. Dragging a dogsled that weighs several hundred pounds through the snow and ice in Alaska, like they do in the Iditarod dog sled race? Now *that* bears a resemblance to real work.

Bonnie Buchanan, a North Carolina dog trainer who trains dogs to act in TV commercials and movies, says, "To them, all of it is play." Partly, that's because she *makes* it fun for the dogs she trains.

Other animals work hard for people, of course. Elephants can pull or carry huge loads; and horses help us and entertain us in everything from wagon-pulling to the Kentucky Derby. But no other animals are expected to do the great variety of tasks that we expect from dogs.

Why do dogs work for us so willingly? Possibly, because they want to please us. But why would they care about pleasing us?

The loyalty of dogs to humans is surely part of the answer.

From farms to battlefields to airports, the loyalty of dogs to humans is a wonderful story. We don't know if they simply want to please us; and we don't know if they consider it work. All we know is, our dogs always seem eager to help us.

# B.a.R.K.-ING IN THE Bay

**1.**

*Crack!*

When baseball superstar Barry Bonds hits a home run out of the San Francisco Giants' new stadium—and into the water of nearby San Francisco Bay—most baseball fans would consider the ball a goner.

But they don't know Rio, the captain of a team called the Baseball Aquatic Retrieval Korps— B.A.R.K.

How could this woolly sixty-pound dog bring together a TV comedian, a major-league baseball team, and an animal shelter that had scores of homeless dogs and cats needing to be adopted?

It sounds complicated, but Rio was up to the job.

Rio, a black Portuguese water dog, was just a pup when he came to live with Pam Marcus in Kensington, California, near San Francisco. Pam, a physical therapist who works with handicapped children at an area hospital, had wanted a dog that wouldn't make her allergies act up. She found out that Portuguese water dogs don't shed their hair and their oily coats don't trigger peoples' allergies.

But what's a water dog?

Bred for many years by fishermen in Portugal, these chunky dogs work in the choppy waves of the ocean. They're trained to jump into the water to help bring in nets and floats, retrieve items that might have fallen off the boats, and carry messages from boat to boat.

To Pam Marcus, Rio sounded like the perfect

pet—an outdoor dog that wouldn't stir up her allergies. She and Rio joined other owners of Portuguese water dogs who met at a nearby lake each summer to give their dogs a workout. "We train them to jump off boats on command, retrieve, work in the water at a distance from us, carry messages from boat to boat, and retrieve things under water," Pam says.

At about the same time, the Giants were building their new baseball stadium on a flat landfill bordering San Francisco Bay. A little inlet of the bay—McCovey Cove—runs outside the right-field wall of the stadium. The team's owners and managers knew that any home run hit over that wall was going to land in the bay.

That's where the TV comedian came in.

Don Novello, star of *Saturday Night Live* and other television comedies, is an avid baseball fan and a dog owner who lives in San Francisco. He suggested that the Giants could use dogs to retrieve the home-run balls hit into the bay. At first the team thought he was just being a comedian . . . but eventually they got in touch with the Portuguese water dog owners, and B.A.R.K. was born.

As the most experienced diver, Pam Marcus's dog Rio is considered the team captain, but he has several doggy teammates: Shadow, known as the fastest diver; Surfer, the youngest "rookie"; Justy, the free spirit; Topper, who seems to sense where every stray baseball is going to land; and Kyma, who cherishes the team spirit and loves diving with Topper.

At midmorning on the day of a weekend home game, the B.A.R.K. team and their owners gather at a nearby boat basin and clamber into a small boat called *The Good Ship Jollipup*. They motor out into McCovey Cove before the baseball teams take their batting practice. The owners can't actually see the game from the cove, so they listen to the game on a portable radio they bring with them, and wait for the announcer to inform them that a home-run ball is sailing over the right-field fence.

When the ball lands in the water, Pam and the other dog owners use hand signals and verbal commands to help the dogs locate it. The dogs are bred and trained to retrieve items in choppy waves that are hard to see over.

Now the question was: What to do with the baseballs that the dogs fish out of the bay? The Giants' management had already figured that one out, and that's why *The Good Ship Jollipup* was waiting out there in McCovey Cove. The boat is owned by two women—Brenda Barnette and Marguerite Judson—who operate Pets In Need, a local animal shelter that provides a temporary home and medical care for abandoned and homeless dogs and cats. The baseballs that are retrieved from the bay are auctioned off to fans, and the Giants provide that money and an additional contribution to Pets In Need.

The publicity provided by B.A.R.K. proved to be a big bonus to Pets In Need. The shelter usually found homes for about fifty abandoned animals a month, but after the B.A.R.K. dogs went to work—and were shown on TV and in the newspapers—the number of adoptions nearly doubled in just two months.

None of this made a huge impression on five-year-old Rio. He's a former show dog who also has won medals in agility and obedience. During baseball's off-season, he often goes with Pam

Marcus to her physical therapy sessions with children. And he trots around her house with a rolled-up sock in his mouth, trying to scare up a game of toss and fetch.

Of course, dogs can round up other things besides baseballs. . . .

# SHEEPISH BEHAVIOR

## 2.

Hazel hunkered down on her belly and made sure everything was in order. She had that alert look that cats get when they lie flat in the grass in order to stalk a bird.

But Hazel wasn't stalking . . . the seven-year-old Border collie was in charge of three dozen sheep at the other end of the corral, and she was in position to enforce her role as The Boss.

Watching Hazel at work is fascinating because she seems to understand instantly what position she needs to be in to get the herd of sheep to do what she wants them to do. Earlier, in a large pasture, she had sprinted uphill at an amazing speed, then moved in a big quarter-circle in order to get a commanding position on a group of sheep below her on the hillside. All she needed to do then was move a few yards to her left in order to get the sheep to move to the right; or go a few yards to her right to get the sheep to move to the left.

Hazel lives on Joey and Angela Judd's farm in central Tennessee. The Judds' hillside farm includes a half-dozen Black Angus cattle and an old swaybacked horse that Joey doesn't have the heart to get rid of. But the farm exists these days for only one purpose: to breed and train Border collies and Australian shepherds to herd sheep and cattle. So the sheep on the farm—about three dozen adults and a dozen cute little lambs—are not there for their wool. They're there so the sheepdogs can learn their jobs.

Sometimes a farmer with a large herd of cattle or sheep will call the Judds and ask them for a trained sheepdog. Or sometimes a farmer will bring a dog to the Judds to be trained. The dogs that Joey and Angela work with wind up all over the country—often in the Western states where the farms are so big and the herds of sheep are so large that the farmers need extra help keeping their livestock together.

Border collies originally came from Scotland and are commonly used as working dogs in this country. They're not that big—about thirty pounds—and they usually have shiny black hair with brilliant white necks, chests, tails, and feet. They're bright-eyed, smart, and fast learners.

The trainers and dog handlers can direct the dogs with verbal commands, by whistling—which comes in handy across a large pasture—or by waving a shepherd's staff, which is about six feet tall, wood or aluminum, with a curved hook at the top.

Hazel's abilities demonstrate how many different herding skills the dogs need to learn:

• Distance: If Hazel is too close to the sheep or too far away, she can't react fast enough if some of the sheep move in the wrong direction. So the sheepdogs learn to stay about thirty to fifty feet behind the sheep, and "direct traffic" from there.

• Speed: Good sheepdogs move quickly but they don't panic the sheep into a gallop—that's the quickest way to injure sheep, particularly when the weather is hot and dry, because the sheep can easily become overheated. Hazel doesn't tolerate any laziness among her sheep, but she doesn't charge toward the herd, either.

• Position: Hazel has a remarkable understanding of the terrain. She knows where the woods are, how the hills and gullies come together, what the wind direction is, and what the sight lines are. She constantly changes position to maintain her control of the herd. When she's got the sheep where she wants them, she flattens down in the grass on her belly, her bright eyes alert for stragglers or wanderers.

In the West, farmers often use bigger dogs, like German shepherds, to protect their herds from wolves and other predators. But even in the East, Joey Judd says, foxes, stray dogs, and occasional wolves can attack sheep and cattle. Border collies and Australian shepherds need to be gutsy as well as brainy.

Hazel's usefulness to Joey Judd isn't limited to pastures and corrals. Long ago he found that when he needed to feed the sheep inside the barn, they'd crowd around and jostle him so frantically that he couldn't feed them efficiently.

He and Hazel devised a neat system: first, Hazel herds the sheep out of the barn; then she stands guard at the barn door, keeping the sheep outside while Joey pours out their food (mostly a corn mix). Then he signals Hazel and she steps aside and lets the hungry sheep stampede back into the barn.

Hazel's jobs on Joey Judd's farm show that Border collies are both smart and versatile—that is, they can do many kinds of jobs, and not all of them involve sheep. . . .

# 3. CLEARED FOR TAKEOFF

It's a good thing that Border collies are high-energy animals, because Jet had a lot of territory to cover.

Jet's job came about because of the location of Southwest Florida International Airport. On a map, you can find it just inland from Fort Myers and north of Naples. Just south of the airport is the Corkscrew Swamp Sanctuary, the Big Cypress National Preserve, and the Everglades National Park . . . bird heaven, in other words.

The closeness of swamps, marshes, state parks, and sanctuaries made the airport, with its runways and acres of grass, an irresistible lure to the thousands of birds in the area. Not only was the airport directly in the path of many birds' migration routes, but many of the birds native to the area are big—herons, egrets, wood storks, and cranes.

When these birds gathered near the runways and collided with planes landing or taking off from the airport, the birds always lost, but the airplanes were likely to be damaged in some way as well. A study by the Federal Aviation Commission showed that collisions with birds had caused $48 million in damage to aircraft in America since 1991. The Florida airport administrators searched for solutions.

What to do?

Jet was a mostly black Border collie, just two years old in 1999. He was living at the Border Collie Rescue Center in Melrose, Florida, where a dog trainer named Nicholas Carter trained collies to chase birds off golf courses. Carter saw a television documentary about "airport dogs" in other parts of the world. He mentioned the idea at a conference he attended in Ohio—and one of the people who heard him was Bobby Orick, operations manager for Southwest Florida International Airport.

Suddenly, Jet was employed. The airport paid $6,000 for one year of Jet's energy, and for Carter to train the dog, and train airport employees in how to handle him. Coincidentally, he'd been given his name long before he became an "airport dog."

The idea was simple: for ninety minutes each morning and ninety minutes each evening—when it's cooler and the birds congregate on airport property to hunt for food—Jet would be unleashed when planes were due to land or take off from a particular runway. Bobby Orick and other airport employees used a sheepherder's whistle (like a referee's whistle) to give Jet his commands. They could even command him to drop to the ground if an airplane was skimming low overhead.

Jet was an instant success. "There's been an

immediate reduction in the bird population" at the airport, Orick said. A report written for the airport administration after Jet had been on duty for a year found that he was "very effective" at reducing the bird activity on airport property.

When he wasn't racing after birds near the airport's runways, Jet could eat and relax at a special kennel operated by the airport for its police canine unit—five dogs that were trained to sniff out narcotics or hazardous materials in travelers' luggage or airport cargo. Jet was taken to and from his job in an airport van. But it wasn't all about the birds. In that part of Florida, Jet also had to be trained to keep an eye out for alligators while he was working.

Right after Christmas 2000, Jet developed a heart problem that ended his bird-chasing days. He went into retirement on the five-acre farm of his favorite handler from the airport. But he'd done such a good job that the airport quickly began searching for another runway dog.

In the summer of 2001 a new bird-chaser went to work at Southwest Florida International Airport. Her name? Radar.

# SNIFFING FOR BLACK DIAMONDS

## 4.

Chewy is a huge, slow-moving, yellow Labrador retriever whose expression tells you that he's not easy to impress. To say that he's calm is an understatement: Chewy looks like he *invented* the word calm.

Niblette, his much younger friend, is just the opposite. She's jumpy, energetic, and eager to play—if only she could figure out a way to jump-start Chewy.

But at age eleven Chewy knows exactly what to get excited about: the same thing that excites the chefs and cooks at the world's best restaurants from Paris to Tokyo—a little black mushroom called a truffle.

Paris and Tokyo are a long way from the hilly farmland in North Carolina where Chewy and Niblette live on fifty-seven acres with their owner, Franklin Garland. But blue-ribbon restaurants around the world are humming with excitement in the middle of winter, when Garland, Chewy, and Niblette harvest one of the world's rarest delicacies.

Chewy leads the way across weedy pastures, through some pine trees, and toward a shallow pond. Niblette typically dashes off in all directions, burning up a few million kilowatts of energy.

Ahead of them is a low row of filbert trees. A filbert isn't your usual kind of tree: it grows about twenty feet high, with dozens of branches that splay out from the ground, and no central tree trunk. But it's what's underground that makes the filbert distinctive and valuable: the tree's roots nurture that scarce black fungus, the truffle.

The truffle is round, black, and about the size of a golf ball. It's a member of the mushroom family, but mushrooms grow aboveground and truffles grow just under the soil. Technically, that makes them a fungus. They grow in the root systems of only a few types of trees—usually filberts, hazelnuts, and oak trees—and only in certain kinds of soil.

Truffles have a powerful aroma but a delicate taste. The world's best chefs treasure them because they bring out the best taste in gourmet foods. If the restaurant is really fancy, and the chef in the kitchen is really demanding, only one kind of truffle will do: the black perigord truffle.

And Chewy knows where they are.

Truffles can grow wild, but because of the worldwide demand, they are cultivated on farms more and more often. But there are only about twenty truffle farms in the United States, and truffles can be harvested for only about two months in the middle of winter. That's when Chewy goes to work. Franklin Garland leads him on a leash out to the filbert trees near the farm's pond. "If he's not on the leash, he won't hunt for them," Garland says. "He knows what he's looking for." Chewy puts his nose to work: Garland has trained him to smell the truffles even though they're not visible above ground. Garland says Chewy was easy to train because truffles have a distinctive smell that he describes as "sweet, nutty, and woodsy."

When Chewy paws gently at the ground, Garland pulls the dog back and digs with his fingers. The truffles he finds are soft and tender, and look like black walnuts.

From a few dozen filbert trees, and harvesting them only in two months during the winter, Franklin Garland can find only about fifty pounds of truffles a year. Seems hardly worth the effort, doesn't it? Until you figure that truffles are so rare, and so highly sought after by gourmet cooks, that chefs and restaurants and specialty-food stores normally pay at least $1,000 per pound for them.

You do the math: if Chewy and Franklin Garland can turn up fifty pounds of truffles in two months, and restaurants will pay them $1,000 per pound for the little black balls . . . that makes Chewy's nose an extremely valuable piece of property.

And Garland is training Niblette as a truffle-finder, too, if he can get her to hold still for a minute. "She's pretty good," he says; "she's almost ready to go on her own." Meanwhile, he's planting more filbert trees so he can expand his truffle business. In fact, he plans to sell filbert trees as well as selling truffles.

From their modern wood-and-stone house, and the two greenhouses nearby, Franklin Garland and his wife Betty clean, package, and ship the truffles all over the United States and overseas. Thanks to these rare mushrooms, this black-bearded, fifty-year-old farmer communicates regularly with world-class chefs, and once appeared with Chewy on the David Letterman show. Letterman had a surprise for them—before the show, he put a truffle in the pocket of his suit jacket . . . and then was amazed when Chewy strolled right over to him during the broadcast and began sniffing at his pocket.

Garland's interest in truffles was sparked by a

*Wall Street Journal* article he read about them in 1978. He and his father spent years traveling around the United States and Europe researching truffles and how to cultivate them.

Until recently, truffles were mostly a European delicacy, grown in France and Italy. For generations, European farmers have used pigs to find and dig out the truffles. But truffle farmers in the United States find dogs easier to work with; Garland got Chewy when he was eight months old (he was already named for Chewbacca of *Star Wars* fame because of his shaggy coat). His coat is short now and he certainly doesn't know that the Italian chef Marcella Hazen has said, "A well-trained dog with a talented nose is nearly priceless."

Chewy, though priceless, *still* looks hard to impress.

# THE DOG WHO DIDN'T NEED TO HEAR

## 5.

The busy port city of Juneau is the capital of Alaska. It's located on the Gastineau Channel in the southeastern part of the state.

But seventy years ago, long before Alaska became a state in 1959, Juneau was not much more than a sleepy fishing village at the base of some cloud-covered mountains. The town did have one famous resident who always knew precisely when ships would be arriving. Her name was Patsy Ann. She was a small white bullterrier, and she was born deaf.

What made Patsy Ann so famous that today there's a bronze statue of her in the Juneau harbor?

She was born in Portland, Oregon, in October 1929; no one remembers why she came to Juneau as a puppy. Today we would call her "homeless" because she didn't live with any particular family, but in fact had many homes—restaurants, bars, the lobbies of hotels, and other businesses along the Juneau waterfront. When the Alaskan weather got too cold or too wet, she slept in the Longshoreman's Hall with the town's dockworkers.

Because she belonged to everybody, Patsy Ann was a big eater. Ships' cooks tossed her leftovers; people in bars and restaurants fed her tidbits; and one friend slipped her a candy bar now and then.

Although she was deaf, Patsy Ann had one remarkable talent: she always knew when ships were approaching Juneau, long before they came over the horizon. She'd run down to the harborfront and sit there, waiting to greet them. In fact, she knew more than that: one day when a group of people was given the wrong information about which pier a ship would dock at, Patsy Ann ran to a different pier . . . and guess who was right?

The stories about Patsy Ann claim that she was never wrong about a ship's arrival. Therefore, in 1934, the Juneau mayor declared the little bullterrier "the official greeter of Juneau, Alaska." She became the most famous pooch in the West, and had her picture taken more often than the movie star dog Rin-Tin-Tin.

Because she occasionally plunged into the icy Alaskan waters, Patsy Ann developed rheumatism as she grew older—a stiffening of her joints that is like arthritis. When she died in March 1942, a group of her old waterfront pals made her a small coffin and buried her in the Gastineau Channel at Juneau's harbor.

Her fame grew even after she died, and fifty years later, her admirers unveiled a statue to her, sculpted by Anna Burke Harris of New Mexico. Clippings of dog hair from all over the world were included in the bronze statue when it was cast. Today, the statue sits on the wharf at the Juneau harbor, and Patsy Ann's "spirit" can greet cargo ships, fishing boats, and cruise liners just as she did back in the 1930s.

# THE PET TRACKERS
## 6.

When your dog or cat or parakeet is missing, you probably feel so sad it's hard to concentrate on anything else.

That's the way Kathy Albrecht felt a few years ago when her bloodhound A. J. got out of his fenced yard and ran away from home. Bloodhounds, after all, are supposed to *find* things, not go missing themselves. But Kathy had bought A. J. as a pup and, she says, "he was like a child to me."

Kathy Albrecht—she likes to be called Kat— lived on the edge of a redwood forest near Santa Cruz, California. She's a former police officer who had worked for six years with police dogs in the campus police department at the University of California at Santa Cruz.

Kat already owned a playful gray rottweiler named Rachel, whom she had trained for search and rescue missions. She knew that Rachel wasn't experienced enough yet to track down A. J., but she had also trained a friend's golden retriever, Kea. "I knew that if we gave A. J.'s bedding to Kea and told her to 'Take scent, find!' she would understand that we wanted her to find A. J."

She did. Within an hour Kea found A. J., romping happily through the woods near a creek, blissfully unaware of Kat's concern for him.

And that gave Kat Albrecht an idea.

Kat knew that dogs, cats, and other pets go missing from people's homes all the time. And just like her, the owners of those pets are deeply upset until they get their animals back.

So why not train pets to find other pets? Specifically, why not use dogs that are already trained to follow scents to track down and find missing pets?

Kat Albrecht formed Pet Hunters in Santa Cruz, and Rachel, the former police dog, had a new job: find those missing pets when their owners called for assistance. A. J. helps out, too—he used his nose to find a missing cat named Marmalade within minutes. He tracked down missing dogs and recovered a missing Jack Russell terrier named Bubba.

Kat Albrecht and Rachel have performed hundreds of searches for missing pets, and have better than a seventy percent success rate. That is, they can find at least seven of every ten missing pets that they go looking for.

Rachel travels in a spacious cage in the back of Kat's van. Like good detectives everywhere, the two begin a case by interviewing the owner of the missing pet. Kat asks questions about when and where the missing pet was last seen, what the missing pet looks like, and why it might have left home. Then Kat must take into consideration all the other factors: the time of year, the weather, the location (city or countryside), the wind direction, and so on.

Given all these factors—and how small many pets are—Kat and Rachel's success rate is really remarkable. Pretty soon, Kat Albrecht was getting telephone calls for help from hundreds of miles away—much farther than she was realistically able to travel. And an acquaintance of hers was opening a second "pet detective" agency—on the other side of America.

## OLD-FASHIONED DETECTIVE WORK

# 7.

At Redington Shores, Florida, on the Gulf of Mexico near St. Petersburg, two experienced detectives were joining forces. Captain Larry Maynard owned a private investigative agency licensed by the state, and a beautiful tan German shepherd named Libby was retiring from police work for health reasons.

Libby was only a year old; she had been trained for Human Search and Rescue work and she was particularly good at searching for missing people in wilderness areas. But she accidentally swallowed some rat poison, and the diseases and infections that followed made it impossible for her to continue searching in rugged country.

Larry Maynard had heard of Kat Albrecht's work through a mutual friend, and he contacted her through Kat's website. His work as a private detective meant he could bring modern technical methods to the job of locating missing pets. Not only did he acquire Libby, he also established a computerized pet registration service, a computerized database, and links to animal welfare agencies and veterinarians.

As he and Libby got into the job of tracking down missing pets, they found that, as Maynard put it, "it's all detective work." That is, basic police methods still get results. Like Kat Albrecht, when they're called onto a case, they begin by interviewing the missing pet's owners and then decide where to start.

Maynard had trained hunting dogs, so he already knew that search dogs work on "scent discrimination"—which means they have the ability to locate and follow a single scent despite all the distractions of other smells from animals, cars, people, buildings, nature, and so on. Maynard and Libby work in all kinds of areas—cities, suburbs, and the countryside. They've tracked all kinds of pets, including horses, and Maynard has noticed some differences: "A lost cat will stay close to home . . . we'll find them in a neighbor's yard or up a tree. But a runaway dog can cover thirty miles in a day or two if he really wants to."

Teamwork really counts in tracking stolen horses, Maynard says. Libby can track the horse as long as it's on foot—or hoof. But when the missing horse gets put into a van or trailer, Maynard's traditional police and detective work will take over. He'll try to locate witnesses, broadcast the missing horse's description, and comb police files for similar crimes in the past.

Libby, now four years old, found almost forty missing pets in her first few months on the job. She and Maynard travel almost every day of the week, but try to restrict their operations to within the state of Florida. Because he gets so many calls for help, Maynard has recently trained two additional teams as pet detectives: another in Florida and one in Washington, D.C.

Maynard and Kat Albrecht have the same advice for pet owners: the smarter you are about putting collars and tags on your pets, the less likely it is that you'll have to call on Libby and Rachel to do their jobs. Both Larry Maynard and Kat Albrecht hope that you *don't* have to call them.

## TOP DOG ON CAMPUS

# 8.

How does sitting outside on a fall afternoon,
watching a college football game, getting tickled
under the chin by pretty cheerleaders, being adored
by half the state of Georgia, appearing in a movie
now and then, and chilling out in an air-conditioned

doghouse sound to you?

Does this sound like work?

Not exactly. But some dogs have all the luck. Since 1956, the University of Georgia mascot has been a bulldog named Uga (pronounced ug-ah)— six of them, actually, one after the other. The Ugas have been called the nation's best-known mascot. They've appeared on the cover of *Sports Illustrated*, in *Time* and *Newsweek* magazines, on network television, at many football bowl games, in the Georgia Senate and the Georgia House of Representatives, and in the Georgia governor's office. Not bad for a chunky little animal that doesn't even come up to your knee.

How did this come about?

College students and school sports fans are known to go a little bit bananas over their team's mascots. This is a kind of "school spirit" that can take hold of just about anyone, lawyers included.

In 1956, a young law school student named Frank W. "Sonny" Seiler was working in the University of Georgia ticket office for sports events when a classmate gave his wife Cecelia a white English bulldog that he had named Uga, for the

"U" of Georgia (GA). The dog became Uga I, appearing as a mascot at the university's football games. He wore a spiked collar, and Cecelia Seiler made his little red shirts out of her children's cast-off T-shirts. Because the university's sports teams are called the Bulldogs, Uga was in constant demand.

Gradually the dog began to appear at more and more events—basketball games, social functions for the university's graduates, the university law school, business school, and veterinary school. He began to travel to the football team's out-of-state games, as well as those in Georgia. And although Sonny and Cecelia Seiler moved back to his hometown of Savannah after he graduated from law school, Uga traveled almost every week-end to the university's main campus in Athens, Georgia.

By the time Uga II took over from his bulldog father in 1966, scheduling the dog's appearances was nearly a full-time job. Seiler's son Charles gradually took over the task of driving the dog to out-of-state sports events. And pretty soon Uga's red shirts were being custom-tailored from the same material as the football team's game jerseys. Sonny and Cecelia established certain standards for the Uga mascots: they had to be English bulldogs; they had to be registered as purebred dogs with the American Kennel Club; and they had to be white. Red and white, after all, are the University of Georgia colors.

There was only one problem: Georgia weather.

Even in the fall, Georgia weather is hot, and English bulldogs don't tolerate the heat very well. The Bahamian Bulldog Club of Nassau, in the Bahama Islands, came to the rescue by providing an air-conditioned doghouse for Uga on the football field. Now Uga was really on a roll.

Uga bulldogs have made special appearances for the March of Dimes, the Easter Seals campaign, and the American Cancer Society. They've appeared in the Rose Bowl parade and other bowl game parades, and in the Savannah St. Patrick's Day Parade.

It's a good thing the English bulldog is such a calm, placid animal. "These dogs have a wonderful disposition," Seiler says. "We now have six grandchildren and the dogs are just great with them."

The dogs grow up accustomed to being around noisy crowds.

When Uga number five was supervising the university, Hollywood came calling. The movie *Midnight in the Garden of Good and Evil* was being filmed in Savannah, Uga's hometown. It's a murder mystery and courtroom drama, and Seiler, the lawyer who has owned all the Uga bulldogs, plays a judge in the movie. Uga number five has two appearances in the movie, one near the beginning and one near the end, almost upstaging the movie's costars, John Cusack and Kevin Spacey. And Seiler's law office appears in one scene, the walls covered with red-and-white portraits of the various Uga mascots, one through six.

When older Ugas die, they're buried in a special location inside the university football stadium, with a little bronze plaque to honor each one. The current Uga is about four years old now, and the biggest of them all at a hefty fifty-five pounds. Like those before him, his permanent home is in Savannah with Sonny and Cecelia Seiler, and he travels constantly to University of Georgia events with their son Charles.

All this may sound a bit extreme if you're not a University of Georgia fan, but nothing is too good for their mascot—not even an air-conditioned doghouse.

# a Nose For safety

## 9.

Possy came bounding out of her kennel, eyes bright, mouth open, her ears pricked up, as if sniffing out deadly explosives was the most fun she could possibly imagine.

She was held on a short leash by Airport Police

Officer David Hodge, who knew that this was just a test—a demonstration of Possy's ability to detect dangerous materials in airport cargo or luggage. They were in the enormous garage at Nashville International Airport used by the airport's giant yellow fire engines and other emergency equipment. The tan, short-haired Belgian Malinois was dwarfed by the trucks—their tires came up to David Hodge's shoulders.

Possy didn't waste any time. On the short leash, she practically pulled Officer Hodge around the room, poking her eager nose between lockers full of firemen's suits and huge crates of equipment.

Somewhere in this cavernous room, Hodge and his boss, Captain Don Witherspoon, had hidden a plastic package that imitates the odor of explosive material. In fact, most explosives share a common chemical base, so the same smell can lead to virtually all the different types of explosives.

If you've got a nose as clever as Possy's, that is.

It took no more than a minute for Possy to detect the spot where Witherspoon and Hodge had hidden the test package. When she found it, you'd expect her to jump up and down and bark and yelp with excitement. Instead, she did just the opposite: she sat down calmly and quietly as if she was totally bored.

And that's how airport police officers knew she had found something dangerous.

Witherspoon explained that this is a key part of the dogs' training: "They're trained to do the opposite of their natural instinct—just sit down quietly and let the officer take over." Hodge reached behind a cabinet where Possy had found the test package, and gave the dog a small treat from his pocket as a reward. The test package looked like a clear plastic baggie with a lump of clay inside it.

Possy and Hodge are part of the three teams of handlers and dogs at the Nashville airport. The dogs live in a kennel built onto one side of the huge hangarlike building where the airport's fire engines and ambulances are kept. Although you might never see them, teams like this exist at every major airport in the United States.

Federal aviation laws dictate what the airlines must do to protect travelers. They set standards for the equipment that planes must carry, like seat

belts and oxygen masks and fire-resistant uphol-
stery on the seats. Airports must also do their part
for the safety of passengers, like the security
stations at each boarding area where carry-on
luggage is x-rayed.

The dogs at all major airports are a part of these
safety precautions. Some dogs are trained to sniff
out explosives, and some are trained to sniff out
illegal drugs. There are different teams of dogs for
each purpose, because the training is different for
each illegal or dangerous scent.

Early in the year 2001, a virus in England and
other parts of Europe was killing thousands of
cattle. It was called foot-and-mouth disease, and
American agriculture experts were concerned that
the virus could be brought into this country.
Because the United States has vast numbers of
beef and dairy cattle, the virus could do enormous
damage.

Therefore, at a few airports (mostly on the East
Coast, where travelers arrived from England and
other parts of Europe) officials posted dogs that
were specially trained to sniff out food in
passengers' luggage, or shoes and boots that might

be carrying mud or dirt from European farms. At Dulles International Airport near Washington, D.C., beagles were used on this "sniffing duty." When they detected a suspicious odor, the passenger could be pulled aside to have his boots or shoes disinfected, or his suitcases examined for food that might be carrying the virus.

Captain Don Witherspoon explained why the dogs' training is such a complicated business: "Almost all the airport safety dogs are trained in San Antonio, Texas," he said. "But only about one in every one thousand dogs is good enough to 'graduate' from the training program."

He favors the Belgian dogs for this work because they work fast, they're agile, and they can detect suspicious odors from twenty-five to thirty feet away. They look like small German shepherds and weigh about forty pounds. Many airports use German shepherds or Labrador retrievers. Agility is important because dangerous materials, from drugs to explosives, can come in very small packages that can be hidden almost anywhere.

The Texas training program for these dogs is long—about thirteen months—and when the dogs are assigned to a given airport, they must go through another three months of training and adjusting to the smells at their particular location. There's a big difference, for example, between the odors at the Miami airport, at sea level in Florida, and the Denver airport, a mile high in the Rocky Mountains. The dogs need to learn not to be distracted by the many smells that drift around in all airports: air-conditioner ducts, restaurants and kitchens, passengers' perfumes, and so on.

The dogs' handlers receive extensive training, too. Witherspoon, for example, was trained in Alabama as a bomb-disarmament technician. The handlers learn that the dogs are clever enough to fool them—the dog might sit down and pretend to discover something just in order to get a little reward. The handlers also learn to keep their hands and uniforms clean, so they don't carry a suspicious odor and confuse the dogs.

Witherspoon and Hodge have found that Possy and her airport companions are a popular act in other locations, too—they've demonstrated their skills in classrooms ranging from elementary schools to universities.

By the time Possy was back in her kennel at the airport, the sound of jets taking off was a distant roar, and the passengers on those planes were just getting comfortable in their seats. Do you suppose she knew that she was partly responsible for their safety?

# THE PICK OF THE LITTER

## 10.

Five years ago, when Ian Russell went to pick out a Border collie from a litter of pups at a breeder's kennel in Winnipeg, Manitoba, he had no idea he was about to get a dog that would grab newspaper headlines and TV airtime from one end of Canada to the other.

Russell stared at the little pile of furballs in front of him and picked out one of them based strictly on its unusual color: "The combination of black, brown, and white hair is very rare on a Border collie," he explains. He took the pup home to his wife, Lesley, and their twins, Sam and Susan. The kids named the dog Bingo.

The twins at that time were barely three years old; they had an older brother, Sean, and two older sisters, Andrea and Allyson. To keep the kids entertained indoors during the long Canadian winters, the Russells kept a small wagon in the house—and pretty soon they began to notice something weird.

When the twins were in the wagon, Bingo—before he was even six months old—would push the wagon along with his front feet, and lean forward while he was pushing to lick the kids' faces.

Ian Russell began to suspect he had an unusual dog here—in more ways than just its color.

When Bingo was eight months old, Ian borrowed a neon-green skateboard from a friend at work, put Bingo on it, and showed the dog that he could balance on the skateboard with two feet, and push himself along with his other two paws. To the family's amazement, the Border collie caught on immediately.

Russell tried something else, too. "In the kitchen I taught him to pick up an empty ice cream carton and put it in the trash can. Gradually I moved the trash can farther and farther away. Then we went out to public parks in the neighborhood and I got him to pick up litter there, and put it in the trash cans."

The strangest part was yet to come. "I never introduced the skateboard and the litter together— but within five minutes, Bingo could do it." The dog would scoot around on his skateboard picking up trash in the park, and putting it in trash cans.

Needless to say, you can't keep this kind of activity secret—the *Winnipeg Free Press* and other newspapers and TV stations began to take notice. In fact, Russell says, life has gotten just a wee bit hectic now that Canadian TV stations and a British magazine are stopping by to see for themselves.

Winnipeg is a thriving city of about 650,000 people, a few hours north of Fargo, North Dakota. The Russell family lives in a large neighborhood with abundant parks and playgrounds, eight schools, and an active community center. Bingo, who's now four, "has really grown up with the twins," Russell says.

And the dog continues to amaze everyone around him. On a Canadian TV show called *Pet Projects*, Ian took Bingo to a neighborhood ice cream parlor, and had the dog put five dollars on the counter. Bingo then took his ice cream outside onto a patio, and when he had licked the plate clean, took the empty plate to the nearest trash can.

Don't believe it? Neither does anyone else— but it's all on film. In fact, the mayor of Winnipeg, Glen Murray, jokes that "Bingo is my skateboard instructor."

Ian Russell doesn't really have an explanation for Bingo's cleanliness and need for speed. His sister trains Border collies for agility trials, but Russell reports, "I've always had retrievers before this." All he can say is that Border collies "are very intelligent, very sensitive dogs who just live to please."

Now if the twins can just train him to do their homework. . . .

# STUBBY THE SPY CATCHER AND OTHER WAR HEROES

## II.

In the summer of 1917, soon after the United States had joined England and France against Germany in World War I, a little stray bullterrier was adopted as a mascot by the Army's 102nd Infantry Division in the United States.

# Stubby the Spy Catcher

When the soldiers shipped out for France aboard a steamship, they smuggled their little friend—named Stubby—aboard the ship by pulling him through a porthole. In France, Stubby slept with the soldiers in their trenches.

Late one night Stubby woke up with a growl and dashed off. The men with him heard a frightened yell—and one of Stubby's friends, a soldier named Robert Conroy, ran through the trench to investigate.

He found Stubby biting down hard on the backside of a German spy. The American soldiers quickly arrested the spy, but it took a while to persuade Stubby to let go of the German's rear end.

How had Stubby been able to tell the difference—at night—between the scores of American soldiers in the trench and the single German infiltrator? And how did he sense that the spy was dangerous to his American friends?

Whatever that sense is, soldiers have known for thousands of years that dogs can save their lives in many ways on the battlefield. Historians and archaeologists have uncovered evidence that the ancient Egyptians and the ancient Greeks used dogs for guard duty; in Napoleon's army in the early 1800s, a dog named Moustache showed such loyalty and bravery that he was honored by one of Napoleon's generals.

In American military history, soldiers and dogs have depended on each other in virtually every war the country has fought:

During the Civil War, a spirited black-and-white bullterrier tagged along with a regiment of Northern soldiers recruited from a small town in northern Pennsylvania. They called him Jack, and swore that he understood the different bugle calls. Jack stayed with the soldiers on their marches through Maryland and Virginia, and after battles he could locate the dead and wounded from his own regiment.

Jack was wounded at least once and was captured twice by Southern soldiers, but each time he made his way back to his Pennsylvania regiment. After three additional battles, the soldiers collected $75—a lot of money back in the 1860s—to buy Jack a handsome silver collar.

In World War II, during the American invasion of Sicily in 1943, an army dog by the name of Chips was with a patrol of U.S. soldiers as they approached a small outbuilding. When enemy machine-gunfire burst from the building, the soldiers took cover—but not Chips. He raced straight into the building and leaped at an Italian soldier's neck. The soldier and his colleagues promptly surrendered to the U.S. patrol. Although he had a small wound on his head, Chips helped capture ten additional enemy soldiers later the same afternoon.

In the Vietnam War, a German shepherd named Bruiser was leading a patrol with his handler, a soldier named John Flannelly. Bruiser suddenly stopped with his ears up—the "alert" posture that meant the dog had detected enemy troops ahead. When gunfire erupted from the jungle, Flannelly collapsed, shot in the chest. He commanded Bruiser to leave—but the dog wouldn't go. He pulled at Flannelly's shirt until the wounded GI reached up and grabbed Bruiser's harness. Bruiser began to drag his handler away from the fighting. When Flannelly was taken to the nearest field hospital, he refused to be evacuated to a bigger medical center until he was allowed to see Bruiser and was convinced the dog was safe. Their loyalty worked both ways.

Over the years, dogs in the military have served in a variety of roles that they can perform better than humans:

- They're used as scout dogs, walking with their handlers at the head of patrol units to detect suspicious sounds or smells hidden from the soldiers;

- They're used as messenger dogs, racing between army units because they can cross difficult terrain—mountainous rocks or jungles, for instance—much faster than a human can;

- They're used as sentry dogs, guarding military posts, supply depots, and frontline positions.

Dogs have pulled sleds in Alaska and Greenland; sniffed out minefields and other explosives; parachuted into combat zones; flown in helicopters; and carried ammunition through deep snow. During World War II, they were used to guard lonely stretches of shoreline after German submarines had been spotted off the East Coast of America.

Today the American military has about thirteen hundred dogs at bases all over the world. They're trained at Lackland Air Force Base in San Antonio, Texas, along with the dogs that serve civilian airports in the United States.

Naturally, the soldiers who serve with the dogs develop an extremely close bond with them. A few years ago President Clinton signed a new law that allows military and law enforcement officers to adopt the dogs they served with after the dogs have "retired."

This is the dog handlers' chance to repay the loyalty that the dogs have shown them over the years. "You can trust your life with them," says one Vietnam veteran. "They're the best piece of equipment the army ever invested in."

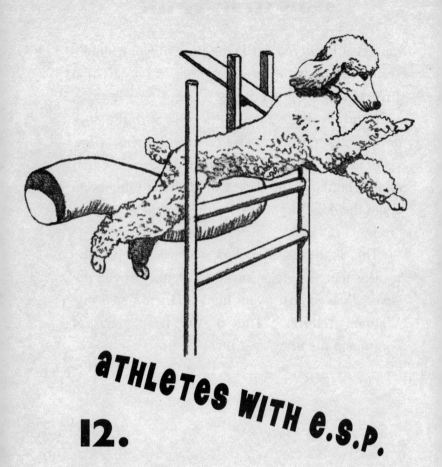

# ATHLETES WITH e.s.p.
## 12.

Who gets your vote as the best athletes in the world?

The basketball players with their spectacular shots?

The soccer players with their dazzling footwork?

The triathletes who need to be good at swimming, running, *and* cycling?

Before you vote, take a look at the dogs who compete in the agility trials that are now held in almost every state.

There's nothing extraordinary about the way these dogs look—retrievers and Chihuahuas, German shepherds and poodles, Border collies and terriers.

But put them on an obstacle course with a variety of fences, tunnels, and other barriers spread out over a few hundred feet, hit the stopwatch— and stand back! It's like punching fast forward.

The dogs in the agility competition race full tilt around an arena—inside or outdoors—that often measures one hundred feet square. Inside the perimeters of this arena are fifteen to twenty obstacles. Some are low fences that the dogs must jump over. Some are A-frames—big wooden triangles set so that the dogs must race up one side and down the other. Some are "dog walks," long narrow platforms that the dogs must race along, three to five feet in the air—not unlike the balance beam in gymnastics. Then throw in an auto tire or hoop, suspended on ropes, that the dogs must jump through. And a seesaw—they charge up one side and down the other as the seesaw tilts from side to side. And a long plastic tunnel—it can be straight or curved like a giant C—that the dogs run through. And don't forget the weave poles—a series of tall flexible poles set so that the dogs must dodge in and out between them at high speed, like the slalom in ski racing.

The fastest dog through the obstacle course is the winner—assuming he or she didn't have any "faults," like knocking down part of a fence while jumping over it.

To make it fair, the dogs are divided into classes based on their size, measured from the ground to their shoulders. At a given agility trial, there may be ten classes, from the littlest Chihuahuas to the biggest German shepherds. And there are three levels of competition: the novice class, for the beginners; the open class, for experienced dogs; and the excellent class, for the real speed demons.

Spike, for instance.

Spike is a big fifty-eight-pound poodle, measuring twenty-five inches from the ground to his shoulders. He's got gorgeous woolly black hair. He loves to have his ears scratched, and plunging your fingertips into that thick, curly hair feels warm and wonderful.

About six times a year, Spike heads for an agility meet with his owner and trainer, Jenny Cobb. She does the driving. Jenny is a computer systems expert at Vanderbilt University in Tennessee. She was born in England, where the agility trials, modeled on horse show jumping, got started in 1978.

What's a typical day like at one of these meets? Let's travel with Spike and Jenny to a competition they attended in Huntsville, Alabama.

The judge for the event sets up the obstacles ahead of time—usually fifteen to twenty barriers, set about fifteen to twenty feet apart. Five minutes before the meet begins, the judge hands out diagrams of the course to the handlers. The obstacles are numbered on the diagram, in the order in which the dogs must go through them. Now the handlers have five minutes to walk through the course, planning their strategies for how to approach each obstacle.

The judge has also set a minimum time—called the "course time"—that the dogs must meet. At the agility trial in Huntsville, the course time was set at sixty-two seconds. When the handlers return to their dogs, some can choose to let their dogs "warm up" at a practice jump outside the arena. But Jenny stresses that dogs' personalities differ just the way humans' personalities do: "Some dogs like to come right out of their cage and go to the course," she says.

The handlers get ready to run alongside their dogs, giving hand signals to the dogs to tell them where to turn and which obstacle is next. Jenny Cobb cautions that hand signals are often not enough. "Sometimes your arm points one way, but your body is facing a different direction. You should use your whole body, particularly your shoulders, to avoid confusing the dog."

The handlers need to remember other rules, too: the teams will not use a leash, and in most meets the dogs will not even wear a collar. The handlers can't touch their dogs during the competition, or they'll be disqualified. And they can't swear or fuss at their dogs.

The judge stands out in the middle of the arena where he or she can have a clear view of the dogs and the obstacles. The timer punches the stopwatch—and Spike is off and running!

A low fence right at the start line is the first obstacle; the second obstacle—twenty feet ahead of them—is a long plastic tunnel through which Spike dashes. Then they turn to the right and Spike races up and down the sides of the tall wooden triangle. Twenty feet ahead of them now is obstacle number four, another low fence. They bear to the left—with Jenny using her body language to guide Spike—and jump another low fence, barrier number five. Turning left again is obstacle number six, a long fabric chute that Spike races through. Number seven ahead of him now is another fence to jump; then the two make a sharp left turn to a triple jump, a higher fence. Another left turn, and Spike accelerates toward the seesaw, obstacle number nine. Turning left again, twenty feet away is another barrier he must jump; and twenty feet beyond that, number eleven is a long plastic tunnel that curves to the left.

Spike's long legs eat up the distance, but the

clock is ticking. Obstacle number twelve is the weave poles, a series of ten or fifteen poles—about three feet high—set close together in a line. The dogs must pass the first pole with their left shoulders, then weave back and forth between the poles at top speed. Jenny says this is the hardest obstacle to train a dog for, but to the people watching, it's the most spectacular. The fastest dogs dodge through these weave poles at lightning speed.

Turning a sharp left now, Spike and Jenny come to the pause table. This is a square table that can be adjusted higher or lower for the different sizes of dogs. The dog is required to jump up onto the table, and the judge signals the handler to have the dog sit or lie on the table for five seconds. The pause table is partly a test of the dog and handler's teamwork, but mostly a safety factor, to make the dog rest for a few seconds.

When the judge signals that the five seconds are up—bang!—Spike and Jenny sprint twenty feet to obstacle number fourteen, a jump fence; and then number fifteen, the dog walk, like the balance beam. Spike runs along the narrow wooden platform, set several feet above the ground, as fast as he dares. When he gets down, he and Jenny turn left again; ahead of them are four fences he must jump, as fast as he can gallop—the stopwatch is still ticking!

Spike sails over the fences—sixteen, seventeen, and eighteen—turns sharp left, and attacks number nineteen, a fence set right at the finish line.

He and Jenny cross the finish line with their hearts pounding, both of them out of breath.

What's the clock say? 57.07 seconds. . . . Spike did the course five seconds faster than the judge's minimum course time!

Which explains why Spike runs in the excellent class. And it's more amazing because of Spike's size—the big dogs aren't necessarily the fastest. They have a hard time getting through those weave poles. Usually the middle-sized dogs—like Jenny's Border collie, Trip—are the fastest overall. At three years old, Trip is a novice dog—a beginner—who's just learning the game.

Jenny says you can start training the dogs as puppies, but the dogs aren't allowed to compete until they're at least eighteen months old, as a way of protecting them against injuries. "The dogs learn in no time," she says. "It takes the handlers longer to learn."

She says it can take a full year for the handler to learn how to approach a course; and a second year for the dog to learn how to take the obstacles, turn, and accelerate. And then it will take a third full year for the team to really learn to work together well. "The dogs need confidence as well as athleticism," she says.

The handlers must also learn the dogs' personalities and preferences. "Spike likes me to leave the starting line right beside him," she says. "But Trip is too fast"—he comes off the starting line like a drag racer—"I need to get way out in front of him in the arena, or I'll never catch up with him."

The dogs become so attuned to working as a team, Jenny says, that "sometimes you'll cross the finish line and the dog will look at you like, 'How'd we do?' They can sense when you're not working together well." But when everything goes right, she says, "Wow! What a thrill! It's like there's extrasensory perception between the dog and the handler. You're not even aware that you're communicating."

While Spike takes a break, Trip will get his chance. For the younger dogs and the novices, a different course will be used: fewer obstacles and slightly easier ones, and a longer time allowance. Nobody knows quite what to expect from the beginners.

However . . .

Jenny's black-and-white Border collie Trip is half the size of Spike, and just getting started in competition at age three. The judge's course time for the novices is eighty seconds. Trip streaks through the course in forty-one seconds.

Maybe Trip has some potential at this stuff.

# STARS OF THE SILVER SCREEN

# 13.

A German shepherd mother and her five pups shivered with fear in the corner of a bombed-out bunker in France. They didn't know what to expect from the American airmen who had just discovered them.

This was in September 1918, just after the end of World War I, and the Americans from the 136th Aero Division were looking for a new place to locate their field headquarters. What they found, instead, was the homeless pup who was destined to become one of the most famous four-legged movie actors of all time.

One of the Americans, a corporal named Lee Duncan, was a soft touch when it came to animals. When he was shipped home to the United States, he managed to bring two of the little German shepherd pups with him. He named one of them Rin-Tin-Tin, after the small dolls he had seen French soldiers playing with during the war.

American movie-goers already had a warm place in their hearts for canine actors. A collie named Jean and a German shepherd named Strongheart were popular film actors before 1920. But when Rin-Tin-Tin made his movie debut in 1922, he made movie history as a handsome, broad-chested four-year-old.

With Lee Duncan as his owner and trainer, Rin-Tin-Tin made at least twenty-seven movies over the next ten years. Within a few years Rin-Tin-Tin was earning $1,000 a week—at a time when almost nobody in America was earning anything close to that. Thanks to his action-packed movie hits, he had his own limousine and his own chauffeur, a diamond-studded collar, and fancy steaks for dinner. He was under contract to the Warner Brothers studio, and movie legend says that the dog's popularity kept the studio financially healthy during its early years.

Rin-Tin-Tin did most of his own action stunts in the movies. Studio technicians said the dog could stand stock-still for thirty minutes without moving a muscle while they set up the lights and cameras for a scene. He starred in a long line of Westerns, mysteries, war stories, and romantic comedies with famous actors such as Wallace Beery and Hoot Gibson.

Rin-Tin-Tin made his last movie in 1931 and died a year later at age fourteen. But he paved the way for generations of doggy movie stars. Lassie was probably the most famous, both in the movies and on TV. Scooby Doo and Goofy have been the big stars of animated cartoon comedies. The popularity of the *101 Dalmatians* movies helped to sell everything from T-shirts to school supplies.

Lee Duncan claimed that he never trained Rin-Tin-Tin. "A trained or broken dog wears a look of fear while he is performing his set tricks," he said. "Rin-Tin-Tin has never felt a whip. We simply understand each other, and until you understand your dog you can never hope to teach him anything."

# TOGA AND GRACIE
# 14.

Gracie reminds you of the kid who's waiting to be asked to tell jokes at the grown-ups' dinner party. She's a black-and-white Border collie, six years old going on three, and just bursting to show you what she can do.

# Toga and Gracie

What she can do will amaze you. In a high-speed blur, she opens the doors of a toy refrigerator, opens a mailbox and takes a letter out in her mouth, opens the door to a child's playhouse and races inside, then opens the window shutters from inside and pokes her pretty head out with her white paws over the windowsill.

Her energy, her bright eyes, and her perked-up ears help explain why she's been in more than fifty television commercials in the past few years, along with countless plays and personal appearances. She's such a show-biz personality now, she can fly first class on American Airlines as a "celebrity dog," using a seat belt just the way a person does.

All of this is still a bit of a surprise to her owner and trainer, Bonnie Buchanan of Sanford, North Carolina. Bonnie spent twenty-one years as a public school teacher, and always used dogs in her teaching: pictures of dogs, toy dogs, real dogs, whatever would get her students' attention. Then in 1991 she opened a dog training center intending to concentrate on two types of training: obedience training, which she called puppy kindergarten, and agility training, in which dogs race around, over, and through a series of obstacles in a timed competition.

That was the plan—and it lasted almost a full year.

Late one evening in November 1992, Bonnie was locking up her training center after a full day of obedience training, when an assistant discovered a small, hairy, blue bundle at the building's front gate. This scruffy little pup was covered with blue paint—a mystery that Bonnie never figured out—and had a note tied around its neck that said: "Mrs. Buchanan, We know you love little dogs, so please take me."

Bonnie suspected that she was being forced into accepting this little mutt by one of her former school students, but at that hour, she didn't have much choice. She took the dog home, washed the blue paint out of its hair, and planned a next-day trip to the vet to get the dog its shots, and then find it a permanent home. By the next morning, though, the pup *did* have a home—with Bonnie.

The dog's bouncy personality was totally irresistible. Bonnie Buchanan named the dog Toga, and tried to figure out what breed it was. She decided it was a "Can-Ar-Ly," which she says stands for "Can hardly tell." That was the beginning of the way Toga changed Bonnie's life.

The next big change occurred only six months later, when a film studio in Wilmington, North Carolina, called Bonnie to help solve a problem. The movie *Getting In* was being filmed in Wilmington, and the dog trainer on the set couldn't get her dog to do a certain scene. It involved having the dog grab a banner from an actor, pulling and tugging and finally yanking the banner away from the actor.

Bonnie knew that little Toga loved tug-of-war games, so she loaded Toga into the car and drove a couple of hours to Wilmington to show him to the film's director. Toga got the part—and promptly became such a busy and successful dog actor that Bonnie soon added a third service to her training center: Bon-Clyde Canine Professionals, which trains dogs for acting jobs.

Toga, meanwhile, played Cicely Tyson's dog in the CBS feature *The Price of Heaven*, and played a Cuban dog in the movie *El Cine*.

When Bonnie got the Border collie Gracie from

a Canadian family a few years later, she found that her canine activities—agility training, obedience training, and actor training—had outgrown her space in Sanford.

She started an ambitious building program which today includes twenty-two thousand square feet in three adjoining warehouse-sized buildings. She can use one for puppy kindergarten, and a separate one for agility training. Because the buildings are often used for dog shows and agility events, she added a "judges' room" where dog show judges have a big conference table and a large kitchen.

The three training activities bring people and their dogs—or dogs and their people—from huge distances across the United States and Canada— one family even came from Venezuela, in South America. Another family brought its cat—which Bonnie enrolled in puppy kindergarten. "I taught her the same way we do the dogs," she says.

Gracie has proved to be amazingly versatile as an actor . . . and patient. For various roles she's worn vampire wings, a football helmet and shoulder pads, and reindeer antlers and a big red rubber nose. She's appeared in movies, TV commercials, videos made for corporations, and she's posed for greeting cards.

Bonnie has trained animals to focus on their work despite all kinds of distractions. Her dog actors have had to sit on a moving photocopy machine, in a car seat with their front feet on the steering wheel, in a moving shopping cart, and on a raft in a swimming pool. They've filmed on streets and in a noisy Miami shopping mall.

Bonnie and Gracie have learned together. On one of Gracie's first TV commercial assignments in 1998, one of the film crew people held a big black-and-white clapboard in front of Gracie's face waiting for the director to say, "Action!" At which point the clapboard went BAM! inches in front of Gracie's nose. Bonnie recalls, "Both Gracie and I jumped about ten feet." Instead of getting mad, Bonnie did the smart thing: she drove to the movie studios in Wilmington and bought a clapboard, so she could use it in her acting classes to train the dogs about what to expect.

Today, they're busier than ever. Gracie films TV commercials for BellSouth, the telephone company, and NASCAR, the auto racing series. Toga starred in a corporate video that won the Silver Reel Award from the International Television Association. At age eleven, the little Can-Ar-Ly is beginning to ease into retirement. And Bonnie has been teaching dog acting classes from Tennessee to Pennsylvania. "I guess I never really retired from teaching," she says.

## BALTO'S RACE AGAINST DEATH

## 15.

Balto wasn't the biggest or the strongest dogsled puller in Alaska, but he might have been the most determined. Unquestionably, he saved the most lives. The Alaskan Husky pulled dogsleds back in the days when dogsleds were used to deliver mail across the wilderness of northern Alaska.

Balto delivered something a lot more valuable than mail.

Today, the word "diphtheria" is barely a part of our language. Because so many infants are vaccinated against the disease at birth, it's been wiped out in large parts of the world. Not many years ago, however, it was a deadly disease: diphtheria attacks the throat and lungs and can create a false membrane or blockage across the throat, interfering with breathing and swallowing. And it's highly contagious—that is, it spreads fast from person to person.

These characteristics made it unusually dangerous when diphtheria broke out in Nome, Alaska, in the middle of winter in 1925. If you can find Nome on a map of Alaska, you'll understand why any disease is dangerous there.

Nome is on Alaska's Seward Peninsula in the northwestern part of the state. It's not even two hundred miles south of the Arctic Circle, and a lot closer to Russia (across the Bering Strait) than it is to the state's largest city, Anchorage.

So when an outbreak of diphtheria occurred in

late January 1925, Nome was in trouble—
particularly the young children and Inuit Indians,
who had no immunity to the disease. Worst of all,
the city was out of diphtheria serum, the medicine
that could have checked and treated the disease.

In those days, no highways or railroads went
through to Nome—and in the middle of winter,
they'd have been impassable anyway. The city is so
far north that its harbor is iced in, unusable more
than half the year. And although plenty of the life-
saving serum existed in Anchorage, the January
weather had grounded all aircraft flights.

By January 21, three children had died of
diphtheria in Nome, and more cases had been
diagnosed. How could the all-important medicine
reach the cut-off city?

Alaska's history of using dogsled teams came to
the rescue. The diphtheria serum—in a twenty-
pound package wrapped carefully with quilts,
canvas, and furs—was delivered partway by train.
But the rail line ended in a little town called
Nenana, about 675 miles from Nome. From there,
dogsled teams were organized in relays to rush the
medicine to Nome. The temperature was dropping

below zero, and blizzards were sweeping down from the Arctic Circle.

The dogsled teams plunged through the swirling snow and ice, handing the precious package from sled to sled along the way. A dogsled team was lucky to travel thirty miles before it was overcome by exhaustion and the freezing weather. The temperature in inland Alaska was thirty degrees below zero—and falling.

The dogsled teams generally consisted of eight, plus a lead dog, all huskies. The lead dog had to be both strong and intelligent. In addition to guiding the other dogs, the lead dog had to have a good instinct for where the trail was—buried under all that snow—and needed to be alert to wolves, bears, and caribou in the woods.

The teams followed the old Iditarod Trail through the wilderness. The trail had been established back in the 1800s by trappers and gold-rush miners. But on January 30, 1925, the snow drifts along the trail were at least twelve feet high, and the temperatures were dropping to forty degrees below zero. The men on the dogsled teams were harnessing themselves to their sleds to help pull their dog teams through the wilderness. One of them—a young Athabascan Indian—chanted Indian love songs through the blizzard to stay awake and keep his concentration.

By the time the precious serum was handed off to a young dogsled driver named Gunnar Kaasen, the temperature had dropped to nearly fifty degrees below zero. Gunnar chose Balto as his lead dog. Balto was a tough dog but no one had ever thought of him as a good leader. The team fought its way through the blizzard to a safety shelter just 21 miles from Nome, exhausted and nearly frozen—where they found the next driver and his dog team fast asleep!

Gunnar knew the people in Nome were desperate—so he kept Balto in his harness and the team plunged on. The blizzard was now so fierce that a gust of wind blew the sled and the dogs into the air—and the vital package of diphtheria medicine was tossed into the deep snow.

Gunnar had to use precious time to untangle the team's harness and get the sled back on its runners—but where was the medicine? After the hundreds of miles of struggle by so many dogs and men, he couldn't bear the thought that he had lost the package—and that people in Nome would die as a result.

Gunnar searched through the snowbanks with his bare hands . . . until his numb fingertips hit something hard and he emerged with the package of medicine!

Just before dawn on February 2, Balto led his exhausted dogsled team into Nome . . . and the serum was handed to the doctors and nurses who could save hundreds of lives with it. Balto had led his team fifty-three miles through snow drifts, a blinding blizzard, and temperatures that got as low as fifty degrees below zero.

Five people had died of the diphtheria outbreak, and there were twenty-two additional confirmed cases. But once the serum was put to use, there were no more deaths from the disease.

For a few months Balto and the other dogs on his team were celebrities. They toured the country and a producer in Hollywood made a thirty-minute film about their heroic trip: *Balto's Race to Nome.*

But soon the dogs were sold to a showbiz promoter, and they disappeared for two years into the world of sideshows, penny arcades, and traveling carnivals. Finally, in Los Angeles, a businessman from Cleveland, Ohio, found the neglected dogs in a cheap museum. The businessman remembered Balto's bravery and arranged to buy the dogs for $2,000 to move them to Cleveland. But he was given only two weeks to come up with the money, or the deal was off.

Now Balto was on the other side of a race against time. Radio broadcasters and newspapers spread the word about Balto's plight, and people across the United States contributed their nickels and dimes. Schoolchildren, factory workers, and people in restaurants tossed in whatever they could. A kennel club in Ohio provided the final push, and the $2,000 was collected in just ten days.

In March 1927, Balto and six of his dogsled teammates were taken to the Cleveland Zoo. Legend says that fifteen thousand people saw them on their first day on display there. Balto died six years later—but the museums in Cleveland and Anchorage, and a statue of him in New York's Central Park still honor the determined husky's life-saving dash through the Alaskan blizzards seventy-seven years ago.

# THE DOG WHO LEADS TWO LIVES

## 16.

This is the bloodhound who can track fugitives or missing people through tangled wilderness, or find drowned human bodies under five feet of water.

Keep telling yourself that—because he sure doesn't look it.

This is also the bloodhound who snoozes in the offices of St. Joseph's Catholic school in Nashville, occasionally flapping his big tail against the carpet as little kids come in and out with notes for the school staff. He looks like it would be a struggle for him just to stand up, never mind chase after people in dense woods.

But don't let Madison fool you. At seven years old, he's one of the best bloodhounds in the South—even though his "day job" is to be the unofficial greeter and mascot at St. Joseph's school. Around the school's four hundred students in grades kindergarten through the eighth grade, he looks really big.

How big? Well, he's 130 pounds—put three kindergartners on a scale, and you've got Madison. And he can stand up on his hind feet, put his front paws on an adult's shoulders, and look the grown-up straight in the eye.

*That* big.

Madison is owned and trained by Susan Mitchell, an administrative assistant at St. Joseph's church and school. He lives with Susan Mitchell, but during the day he hangs out in her office, dreaming doggy dreams and wagging his tail when passing school kids give him a pat on the head. In fact, Madison was born in the building, in the upstairs apartment of one of the priests at the church.

It's his other life that holds adventure. At least twice a month Susan Mitchell gets a call from a police department or a sheriff's office somewhere in the South—Mississippi, Alabama, Georgia, South Carolina, or Tennessee. She's learned to keep a suitcase packed at all times. When the calls come, she loads Madison into her car, and they're off to try and locate a missing person.

Maybe it's a child who wandered away from home and got lost in the woods.

Maybe it's an elderly adult who got confused and left a nursing home.

Or maybe it's a prisoner who broke out of jail and fled from police.

Most of the time, the law enforcement officials will put several teams of dogs plus handlers on a case. "We'll usually have five adults and maybe four dogs who work together," Susan Mitchell explains. "I'll ask a lot of questions about what we're looking for, and then the handlers divvy up the assignments among us. I put Madison on a thirty-foot leash when we set out."

Although Ms. Mitchell doesn't charge a fee for her bloodhound services, most police departments will pay her travel expenses. "We've got a good reputation," she says of her work with Madison.

Madison and other good trackers work on the principle of scent discrimination—that is, they can pick out and follow the trail of a specific odor despite all the distractions. Imagine a dog with enough concentration to track a single scent through the woods where there may have been deer, possums, and raccoons—scents guaranteed to tempt a dog's nose.

That's how Susan Mitchell got into this business in the first place. "I once saw these dogs being trained, and I was hooked," she says.

A good bloodhound like Madison can even follow an old trail. "We once sent a person through the fairgrounds when the state fair was in progress and the scent was contaminated by hundreds of odors," Ms. Mitchell says. "Then we came back two weeks later when the fair was gone and the fairgrounds were empty, and the dog was *still* able to pick out the individual scent."

Madison and other bloodhounds trust their noses more than their eyes, so Ms. Mitchell says they're "street stupid": "If you're not in control of them, they'll follow their noses right out into a street in the middle of traffic, or walk straight into the side of a car. They get totally focused on the scent they are following."

Madison can tell when someone has been picked up by a car, or went into a telephone booth.

Even rain doesn't wash away a scent, she says; in fact, the rain refreshes the odor the dogs are trying to follow. Madison and other bloodhounds are so good at this that they can even detect the body of a person who has drowned when the body is under five or six feet of water.

Out in Colorado, the people who train tracking dogs like Madison say, "We're the dumb part of the team." What do you think they mean?

Dogs like Madison are so reliable that in some states, the evidence they find can be admitted in court. In rare cases, Ms. Mitchell says, the dog itself may be called into the courtroom, if there is a question about the animal. "When you get a subpoena from the court," she says, "you need to take all the dog's records, documents, and papers with you" to show that the dog is qualified as a competent tracker.

It's the nature of the business, she says, that there are also a lot of "wild goose chases." She and Madison might spend hours tracking through the woods, only to find that the person who's supposedly missing is sitting comfortably in a restaurant somewhere; or the kid who was thought to have run away from home simply went to spend the night with a friend without telling his parents.

Which is not really bad news after all.

With weary legs, Madison and Susan Mitchell will be back in their office at St. Joseph's school the next morning. Susan Mitchell will be at her computer and Madison will take up the rest of the room, stretched out on the carpet.

Those little kids who stop by to scratch him on the head may have no idea how, or where, Madison spent his busy weekend.

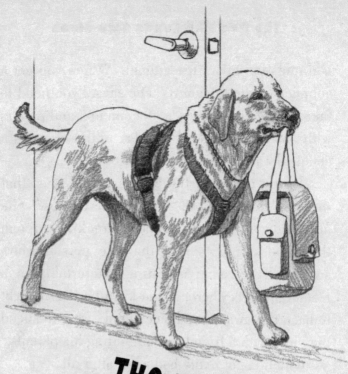

# THE MOST IMPORTANT GIFT

## 17.

Cary, a three-year-old Labrador retriever, can do a lot of things for his human friend Lizzie B. He can open doors for her, pull off her socks, carry her purse or her school supplies, and get her pajamas.

But he's giving her something else that's a lot

more important: independence.

Seven-year-old Lizzie was born with cerebral palsy. The disease affects her speech, her coordination, and her ability to walk and grasp things. But Lizzie has several assets, too— beginning with a dazzling smile and a delightful personality.

And then there's Cary.

Cary is not only a big help to Lizzie, he's a big help to her parents, Ned and Amy Harris-Solomon of Nashville, Tennessee. They no longer feel they need to hover nearby in case Lizzie needs help. They know Cary is on the job: he can do minor chores for Lizzie, like picking up things she might drop. He provides companionship, walking next to her wheelchair at the shopping mall or on their strolls around the neighborhood. Most of all, he provides that growing-up sense of independence— both for Lizzie and her parents. As Lizzie and Cary get older together, they learn the teamwork that enables them to be on their own more and more often.

Being on her own—and not being dependent on Mom and Dad or her older sister, Skye—is important to any seven-year-old. Lizzie, for example, is in the second grade at a Nashville public school. She swims in a neighborhood pool, earns her Girl Scout sew-on patches, and rides horseback when she gets the chance.

Lizzie's parents got Cary from Canine Companions for Independence, an organization in New York State that provides assistance dogs for people with disabilities. Lizzie and her mother spent two weeks in Farmingdale, New York, where Cary was trained, to learn to work efficiently with the dog and issue Cary's commands verbally and with their gestures and body language.

Today, Lizzie and Cary can wander through the mall, fly on jet airplanes, and go into bookstores and restaurants together.

Just a few years ago, service dogs were mostly guide dogs for the blind. Now, all across the country, assistance dogs like Cary are helping people live more normal lives. In Seattle, Washington, an eleven-year-old Golden retriever named Mame helps her owner, Mary Sexton. Mary has cerebral palsy and lupus (an illness that attacks the body's resistance to diseases), but Mame is Mary Sexton's helpful partner in bicycling, skating, skiing, and gardening.

In North Carolina, an eleven-year-old yellow Lab retriever named Murfee has been certified by the American Red Cross as a therapy dog, to help people emotionally, including those who have survived natural disasters like earthquakes or hurricanes. Murfee's owner, Carolyn Uhlin, has found lots of good uses for her dog. She has a master's degree in clinical psychiatric nursing, and she's found that Murfee puts her patients at ease— people who might be tense, angry, confused, or anxious about talking to a psychiatric nurse.

Carolyn Uhlin works in the psychiatric unit of the High Point Regional Hospital in central North Carolina. "Having Murfee with me in the office or clinic makes me more approachable," she says. "The dog helps adults and children stay calm. If it's just me and the patient, it's one thing; but if Murfee is there, the dog will 'break the ice' and it's easier to get people to talk about their problems."

As "comfort dogs" or "therapy dogs," many canines are at work around the country in nursing homes for the elderly, schools for the disabled—

even a cancer clinic where the patients are not confined to hospital beds.

Friendship is just part of what Lizzie gets from Cary. When he's told to "visit," Cary will put his big yellow head on Lizzie's lap, and they'll share a warm-and-furry hug. He sleeps at the foot of her bed at night, and during the day he chases around the grassy lawn outside their house just like dogs everywhere.

But his real gift to the family is that they know they don't have to be a few feet away from Lizzie every minute of every day. Cary and Lizzie are getting to be a very independent team.

# Leaving Prison Behind

## 18.

Everybody loves a story with a happy ending.

This is a story with *two* happy endings.

Dawn Jecs, of Puyallup, Washington, is a dog trainer with a restless mind. About an hour south of Seattle, near Tacoma, she's trained show dogs and agility performers, and conducts regular obedience classes. But she's always looking for new ways of doing things.

Almost twenty years ago, searching for ways to find homes for stray dogs in the Tacoma area, she came up with a creative solution. It would save the lives of hundreds of homeless dogs, provide valuable skills to women in a nearby prison, and train assistance dogs for disabled people in Washington State. It's one of those ideas that's so logical, you can't believe no one ever thought of it before.

First, Dawn began to go through the Humane Society animal shelter in Tacoma, looking for homeless dogs who seemed smart enough, young enough, and lively enough to be trained.

Then, after months and months of wrangling and planning, she got permission to take these homeless dogs into the women's maximum-security prison in Gig Harbor, Washington. Her plan was to train the women prisoners in kennel management, grooming, and other pet-related skills; and at the same time turn the homeless mutts into well-behaved, good-looking dogs that people would want to adopt.

A clever plan. But fate had a lot more in store for Dawn's program than just that.

While Dawn began training the prisoners in kennel management, and the women started training the dogs, Dawn arranged another piece of the puzzle. She understood the need for service dogs to assist the disabled, so she added another program feature: using the prison women to train homeless dogs to help disabled people.

Dawn also understood that after months and months of training and working together, it was hard emotionally for the prisoners to give up their dogs. So she arranged "graduation ceremonies" in which each woman would formally hand over the dog she had trained to a specific disabled individual. Now the prisoners could see the results of their work. And Dawn made sure that each prisoner had a new "project dog" already on the prison grounds, to make it easier for the women to part with their old friends.

Now disabled people in Washington State were benefiting, too.

In the years that her "prison pet partnership" program operated, Dawn uncovered two stars: a prisoner serving a life term named Sue Miller, and a homeless, female German shepherd named Sheba—and Dawn Jecs's good idea was about to get really spooky.

Dawn remembers that, "We were busy training dogs to walk next to wheelchairs, carry backpacks, turn lights on and off, open and close doors, et cetera. Our waiting list was about two years long."

One of the people on that waiting list was a woman named Pat Barnum. She was desperate for help because her thirteen-year-old daughter, Angie, suffered from several seizures every day. During the seizures her breathing would become uneven, she'd fall to the ground, and go into a mild coma or trance. In a few minutes, when the seizure passed and she regained consciousness, some of her memory would be gone.

Someone from Angie's family needed to be with her twenty-four hours a day. The little girl was confined to a wheelchair, wearing a hardhat or a helmet to protect her against injury. She had almost no friends because she was at home most of the time.

As sympathetic as she was, Dawn Jecs could

see no way to help Angie: "What if we did train a dog for Angie and it didn't respond at the right time?" She thought it might be even more dangerous for the girl. Reluctantly, she said no to Angie's mother.

At the same time at the prison, inmate Sue Miller was training a two-year-old German shepherd named Sheba. Although Sheba went home with Dawn Jecs on the weekends, during the week she went everywhere with Sue Miller inside the prison—to classes, to the cafeteria—at night she even slept in Sue Miller's six-foot-by-nine-foot prison room. Sheba was becoming highly attuned to humans.

And Angie Barnum's mom, Pat, just wouldn't take no for an answer. She continued to write to Dawn Jecs, and had Angie's brothers and sisters write. "She bugged us for about a year," Dawn recalls.

So Dawn began to think, What if we provided a service dog for the young girl that would just do all the normal things that an assistance dog can do? Wouldn't that make life easier for the Barnum family?

She invited Angie and her mother to come to the prison to take a look at the dogs and their skills—but nothing could prepare her for what happened next.

Angie had a seizure right in front of the prisoners, the dogs, and the prison staff.

Dawn Jecs recalls: "While everyone was running around attending to Angie, one of the program dogs, Sheba, began to anxiously pull her trainer toward the girl. This dog was usually very quiet and easy to manage, but was insisting on getting closer to the situation.

"Once things settled down a bit, Sheba's trainer, Sue Miller, told me what was happening, and we decided to let Sheba approach Angie. Sheba seemed very concerned about Angie and wanted to stay close to her long after her seizure was over."

Dawn couldn't get the dog's behavior out of her mind. The other dogs had paid no particular attention to Angie during her seizure.

"I guess Pat Barnum's determination had finally paid off," Dawn says. "I decided to give this young woman a trained dog."

Now Angie began to come to the prison

regularly, and as Sue Miller taught her Sheba's commands, the unlikely companions—the life-term prisoner and the young teenager in the wheelchair—formed a close friendship of their own.

As Dawn and Sue Miller trained Sheba in all the service dog skills, they threw in an experiment: they trained Sheba to bark whenever a prison inmate pretended to have a seizure. The dog became 100 percent reliable in this regard. Soon Sheba was ready to make overnight trips to the Barnum house, and began spending weekends with Angie.

The day came when Sheba "graduated" from the prison, and Sue Miller had to say good-bye to her. But Angie's life was changing dramatically: now that she could take Sheba with her, she enjoyed going to school—and she developed lots of new friends there. Also—this is a little surprising—Angie's seizures were becoming less frequent.

As Dawn Jecs remembers it, "One day Angie came in from the backyard where she had been playing with friends and told her mom that Sheba was being naughty, and to please lock her up because she wouldn't let Angie play. Sheba kept getting in her way and interfering with their ball game.

"Before Angie finished her story, she collapsed with a violent seizure. Luckily her mom was there to help her, and eventually the seizure passed." Pat Barnum and Dawn Jecs began to discuss an eerie possibility: Was it possible that Sheba could detect the onset of a seizure before it happened?

Dawn recalls: "When Angie flew east to compete in the Special Olympics, Sheba was at her side. While Angie was competing on the balance beam, Sheba lay next to Pat Barnum in the audience. Suddenly Sheba began to whine and got to her feet and went toward Angie. Pat recognized this immediately and called for Angie to be excused. Although Angie was upset and said she felt fine, she soon showed symptoms of an oncoming seizure. Sheba could obviously detect seizures from a distance, as well as before they occurred."

It's possible that Sheba was the first dog to be deliberately trained as a "seizure alert" dog. But that's not what's important. What is important is that all over the country, a few highly sensitive dogs have been able to alert their owners to impending seizures—saving them from injury or worse.

In Racine, Wisconsin, twelve-year-old Emily was given a Labrador named Watson by the training organization Canine Partners for Life. When Watson senses that Emily is about to have a seizure, he'll whine in a distinct, throaty way— giving Emily time to prepare.

If Emily is sleeping when a seizure seems near, Watson will leave her bedroom, wake up her parents, and then run back to Emily's room. He's been able to push her into a chair when she was about to fall, and once blocked her from an oncoming car when she was having a seizure.

In Galveston, Texas, a young boy named Jacob was having as many as five seizures a day. Like Angie Barnum, his falls were dangerous: he'd broken several teeth and suffered two concussions as he collapsed during seizures.

His parents got Jacob a Lab retriever named Hunter, who had been trained to respond to seizures. But Hunter didn't just respond to an episode that was already happening. Jacob's parents became aware that Hunter would sometimes walk away from Jacob and nudge his mom or dad on the arm. Then he'd stare pointedly at Jacob. Within fifteen minutes the boy would have a seizure. During the seizure, Hunter would lick Jacob's face and lie down next to him.

In Lohman, Missouri, a forty-two-year-old woman named Donna suffered a stroke that partly paralyzed the left side of her body. Over the following few months, she began to have several seizures a day, twitching uncontrollably and falling unconscious.

Donna's husband found her a German shepherd-rottweiler puppy that they named Patra. Patra hadn't been trained as an assistance dog. She developed an odd pattern of head-butting Donna as Donna worked in her garden—or grabbing Donna's sleeve and pulling her down.

Donna and her husband were annoyed, until they realized that each time Patra tried to get her attention, Donna would have a seizure within the next fifteen minutes.

Why? How can dogs do this?

The warning that seizure dogs can give is

critical because today there are medical remedies—like antiseizure pills—that a person can take if they know a seizure is coming on. Donna, for instance, takes Patra to work with her at a computer company. If Patra nudges her arm, Donna simply shuts the door to her office and lies down on the floor until the seizure passes.

Doctors who treat seizure-prone patients, and dog experts like Dawn Jecs, have three theories about how dogs are able to predict seizures in humans. One is that the dogs are aware of very tiny behavioral "clues" from the person—such as a twitching finger or a fluttering eyelid, which are a prelude to an attack.

Another theory results from what an epileptic seizure is: just before the seizure, the neurons in the brain violently increase their electrical discharges. Humans can't sense this in advance, but maybe a very sensitive, people-oriented dog can.

A third theory—this is Dawn Jecs's favorite—is that the unusual brain-wave activity may cause the odor of the person to change; maybe the person is sweating in a way that the dog can detect before the person can. A dog's nose, after all, may be three hundred times more sensitive than a human's.

Medical experts are just beginning to take these stories seriously, designing research studies to figure out why and how dogs can predict human seizures.

Too bad we can't just ask Sheba.

Oh, yes, about those happy endings: Angie Barnum is now in her twenties, married, and living in Tacoma, Washington, with children of her own. And Sue Miller, who trained Sheba, has been paroled from prison, and manages a restaurant in Olympia, Washington. In her spare time she trains assistance dogs for the disabled.

The two unlikely friends, who met when neither of them was truly free, still keep in touch with each other.

# CONCLUSION: THE KING'S LOYAL FRIEND

We can find examples all around us of dogs who work hard and willingly for people, and still we don't understand why. Why would Chewy care about finding truffles with farmer Franklin Garland? Why would Balto push himself to exhaustion through an Alaskan blizzard to deliver life-saving medicine? Why would Bruiser try to pull soldier John Flannelly away from enemy rifle fire in Vietnam?

The only sensible answer we can come up with that fits all these circumstances is loyalty. And the loyalty of dogs to humans is almost as old as written language.

Thousands of years ago, the poet and storyteller Homer wrote down the ancient Greek legend of *Ulysses*.

As Homer told it, Ulysses was a warrior-king who ruled Ithaca, an island kingdom off the west coast of Greece. When he was young, he went off to fight with the Greeks in the Trojan War. Ulysses' victory over the Trojans took ten years, and then he spent another ten years wandering the eastern Mediterranean Sea, in a series of adventures and narrow escapes from mythological monsters.

When Ulysses returned home after twenty years, no one recognized him. He looked a lot different, of course. His former military companions didn't recognize him, merchants and politicians in Ithaca didn't recognize him, even his neighbors and family didn't recognize him.

Except one.

The only one who recognized him, after all those years, was his dog Argos.

Homer's story of Argos' loyalty to Ulysses has endured for over three thousand years. Why would the old storyteller put that little detail about the dog into his long, dramatic poem about Ulysses?

History tells us that Homer was blind. And maybe—just maybe—he had a loyal dog himself.

# acknowledgments

Dog owners are always eager to talk about their pets, but I had something better: Jennifer Cobb of Nashville, Tennessee, who led me to many interesting dog owners and dog trainers around the country. She was the one indispensable source in putting these stories together.

Many other dog owners and trainers cheerfully interrupted their work to answer questions about their working dogs:

Pam Marcus in Kensington, California; Susan Sanders in Fort Myers, Florida; Franklin Garland in Hillsborough, North Carolina; Kathy Albrecht in Clovis, California; Captain Larry Maynard in Redington Beach, Florida; Frank W. Seiler in Savannah, Georgia; Bonnie Buchanan in Sanford, North Carolina; Dawn Jecs in Puyallup, Washington; Ian Russell in Winnipeg, Manitoba, Canada, and Margo Goodhand, features editor of the *Winnipeg Free Press*; Jim Newland in Athens, Georgia; Tony Shaddock in Canberra, Australia; Dana Brynelsen in Vancouver, British Columbia, Canada; Carolyn Uhlin in High Point, North Carolina; and in Nashville, Joey and Angela Judd, Captain Don Witherspoon, Officer David Hodge, Susan Mitchell, and Ned Solomon and Amy Harris-Solomon.

# Sources

B.A.R.K.-ing in the Bay: correspondence and telephone interviews with Pam Marcus; and *DogFancy* magazine issue of January 2001.

Sheepish Behavior: visit with Joey and Angela Judd, April 2001.

Cleared for Takeoff: correspondence and telephone talks with Susan Sanders; and *Naples Daily News* online edition of January 29, 2001.

Sniffing for Black Diamonds: visit with Franklin Garland; and *Greensboro (NC) News & Record* of March 28, 2001.

The Dog Who Didn't Need to Hear: **patsyann.com**, online feature dated May 9, 2001.

The Pet Trackers and Old-Fashioned Detective Work: correspondence and telephone talks with Kathy Albrecht; telephone talks with Captain Larry Maynard; and **nationalpetdetectives.com** website dated March 10, 2001.

Top Dog on Campus: correspondence and telephone talks with Frank W. (Sonny) Seiler; and 2000 University of Georgia football media guide.

A Nose for Safety: visit with Captain Don Witherspoon and Officer David Hodge; *Dog-Fancy* magazine issue of August 2001; and *Nashville Tennessean* of March 15, 2001.

The Pick of the Litter: correspondence and telephone talks with Ian Russell; and the *Winnipeg (Manitoba) Free Press.*

Stubby the Spy Catcher and Other War Heroes: *Smithsonian* magazine issue of December 2000; *Parade* magazine issue of April 1, 2001; and *One Nation Divided*, online magazine dated May 9, 2001.

Athletes with E.S.P.: interviews with Jennifer Cobb, May 2001.

Stars of the Silver Screen: **dogs.about.com** online feature referenced movietvdogs.

Toga and Gracie: visit with Bonnie Buchanan and newsletters of the Bon-Clyde Learning Center.

Balto's Race Against Death: **www.dogsled.com** feature referenced baltohistory.

The Dog Who Leads Two Lives: visit with Susan Mitchell, February 2001.

The Most Important Gift: visit with Solomon family; and Vanderbilt University Register article by Ned Andrew Solomon.

Leaving Prison Behind: correspondence with Dawn Jecs, and *Reader's Digest* issue of October 2000.